CW00894814

If Only They Could Talk

By the same authors

Animal Magic

If Only They Could Talk

Photographs by Mike Hollist

Words by Shaun Usher

CHAPMANS
1990

Chapmans Publishers Ltd
141-143 Drury Lane
London WC2B 5TB

A CIP catalogue record for this book is available from the British Library

ISBN 1-85592-710-1

First published by Chapmans

Copyright © in the photographs Associated Newspapers PLC 1990
Copyright © in the text Shaun Usher 1990

Typeset by The Farnham Printing Company
Printed and bound by The Bath Press, Bath, Avon

'Great to be in your wunnerful country, folks — and
have we got a show for you ...'

'Our claws may look a bit much, but
we'll grow into them.'

'When he lets go, I double in size.'

'I don't care what you three say, this hat is _me_.'

Shared amusement

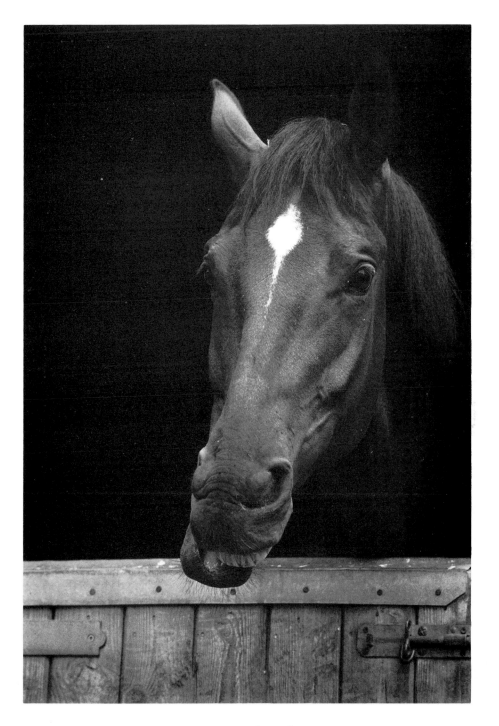

Horse-laugh

Hat Trick

'Tell your fortune, guv?'

Wash

and Brush-up

'No, darling, you're not lanky, you are <u>tall</u>.'

'All one's puppies go through a strange phase.'

'I taught that David Bailey everything he knows.'

*'Try again: dog biscuits, flea collar, rubber bone ...
I knew I should have made a shopping list.'*

Darby and Joan

'Foxy's just a Private — I've got the stripes.'

'She means well, forever knitting, but I wish she'd
make sweaters that fit ...'

Flower / Power

'I'm using the paws control.'

'No, Junior, you can't be a vacuum cleaner
when you grow up.'

'Your bootlace is undone − gotcha, April Fool!'

*'Youngsters should have a flair for
this pesky puzzle...'*

'But it sends me ape!'

Fur & Feather Society

Near the knuckle

'Come and play!'

'Ooh, don't — that *tickles*.'

A quiet joke ...

Boffo laffs.

'Rover's not really panting — I'm a ventriloquist.'

'She's only human, of course — but have you ever
seen such a pathetic beak?'

Behind bars

On the road again

Why the chickens crossed the road

'He's being childish,
it's <u>his</u> turn to push <u>me</u>.'

Who is the fur-est one of all?

Seal of approval

Safe from the hounds

And they say thought can't be photographed ...

'*Tomorrow I start trying this beach-ball.*'

'Yes, very interesting, but you still ought
to see your dentist.'

Said with flowers, sealed with a kiss

Kittenish charm

Big cat

'We really must introduce him to our tailor.'

'Up a bit ... left a bit ... commence refuelling.'

'Pahnd o' seedless, lady? They're luverly!'

' "*Beam me down, Scotty*," *indeed … It's just a bucket, birdbrain!*'

'*We want to join the Cubs.*'

'A word in your ear, young feller ...'

'Forgive me for pointing it out — you've forgotten
to take off the lens cap.'

Beak by jowl

Pecking order

'Ducky and I have a tiny problem with our
Owl and the Pussycat act.'

'It's me again, your MC, the Ray-Ban kid!'

'Are you old enough to be practising acupuncture?'

Lap of luxury

Lap of honour

Togetherness

'I'm sure I left a baby around here somewhere ...'

Featherweight meets heavyweight.

'Nice cap, but the badge could be improved on.'

'I've started, so I'll finish.'

The End